MOM'S DREAM VACATION

written by Pamela Rose

illustrated by Anthony Valbiro

Dedicated to my talented children

Amanda and Robbie

And my dOg-der Zoey

And to all hardworking Moms that
needs a

DREAM VACATION!

School is out for summer

And

Mom is dreaming of a relaxing

vacation...

OUR VACATION

It's a funny thing about moms...they need to have their house spotless before leaving on a vacation.

I guess it's just one of those MOMMY things.

How can you help Mom clean the house before vacation?

Driving to our destination

is always a challenge in

more ways than one.

AWTY
(Are We There Yet)
Got the GPS?
Where's my milk bone?
Mom did you see my I-Phone?
Where's my grande, iced half-caf, low-fat, Carmel latte with whipped cream?

Arriving is a relief except...
I'm thinking the family forgot something??

TO UNPACK THE CAR!
Never fear, Mom is always here.

What can the family do to help mom unpack the car?

AHHHH!
Time to hit the beach and RELAX!

What can the family do to help Mom at the beach?

Night has come kids are asleep and it's time to enjoy a beautiful

starry night...

But mom didn't count on this kind of company!

And when our vacation time is over Mom must make sure the cabin shines from top to bottom.

What can you do to help Mom in the cabin?

MOM NEEDS A VACATION FROM HER VACATION.

A DREAM VACATION!

OUR VACATION

Zoey lead the way!

A shopping spree in New York City with a very lovely lady.

Who is the lovely lady?

What famous buildings can you name in this picture?

Bloomies
FAO
Macy's

Comparing manicures with the Sphinx in Egypt.

What Wonders of the World do you see?

A Can-Can dance in Paris, France.

What is the Mom dancing with?

STOP and smell the roses
in jolly olde England

What is the name of the tower with the big clock?

A gondola ride under a blanket of stars with my best pup.

Where is the only place in the world that you can take this kind of boat ride?

An inspiring conversation
at Mt. Rushmore.

Can you name the four presidents in
this picture?

A red carpet walk in Hollywood?

In what state is Hollywood?

And a Rocky Mountain high…

Where are the Rocky Mountains?

But the BEST memories of all is the time MOM spends with her family.

Answer Key:

The Statue of Liberty, Empire State Building, Chrysler Building

Pyramids

The Eiffel Tower

Big Ben

Venice, Italy

Washington, Jefferson, Roosevelt, Lincoln

California

Colorado

Pamela Rose

Pamela Rose author of "Mom's Time Out"

is now going on a "Dream Vacation."

She is a Jill of all trades: author, art teacher,

artist, radio show host and has

her hand in many aspects of the arts.

As a busy woman of the 21st century,

full time mom and caregiver she thought

moms would like to dream along with her

and travel the world.

Visit my website: momstimeout.net